WHAT ON EARTH?

ROBOTS

Jenny Fretland VanVoorst

Pau Morgan

QED

Contents

See how to use your senses like a robot on page 26.

Read about ancient robots on page 8.

Make your own mechanical grabber on page 20.

Find out about robot jobs on page 48.

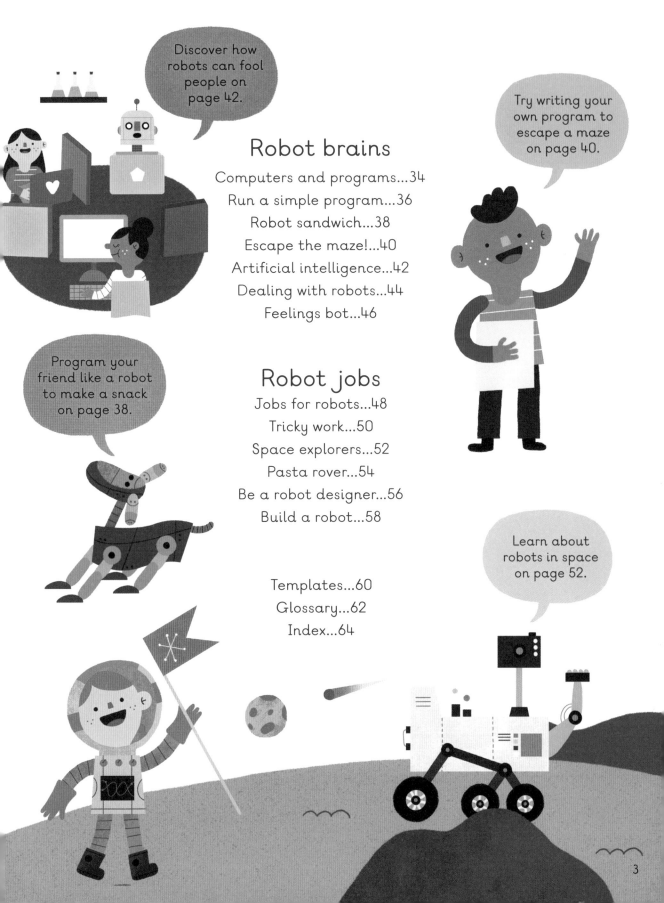

Discover how robots can fool people on page 42.

Try writing your own program to escape a maze on page 40.

Robot brains

Program your friend like a robot to make a snack on page 38.

Robot jobs

Learn about robots in space on page 52.

Robot poetry

What do you know about robots? Can you write your own poem about a robot?

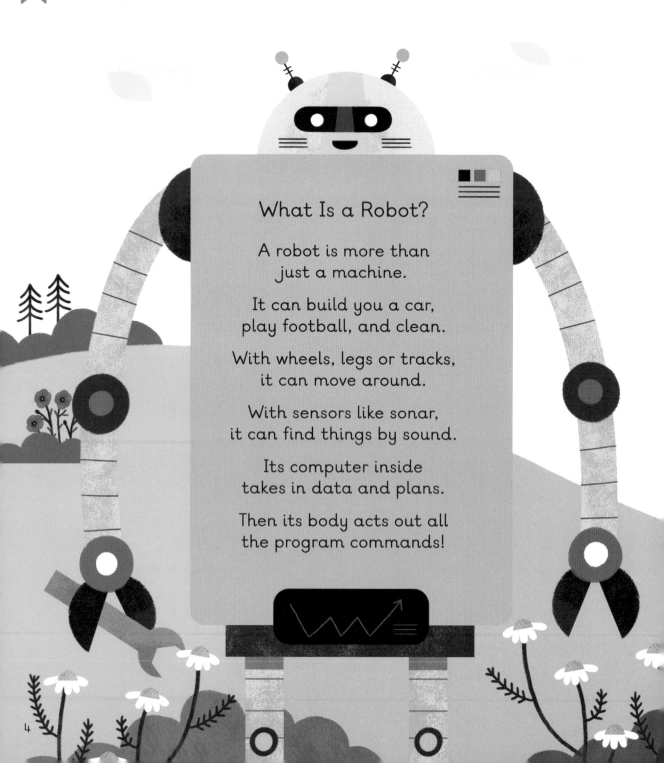

What Is a Robot?

A robot is more than
just a machine.

It can build you a car,
play football, and clean.

With wheels, legs or tracks,
it can move around.

With sensors like sonar,
it can find things by sound.

Its computer inside
takes in data and plans.

Then its body acts out all
the program commands!

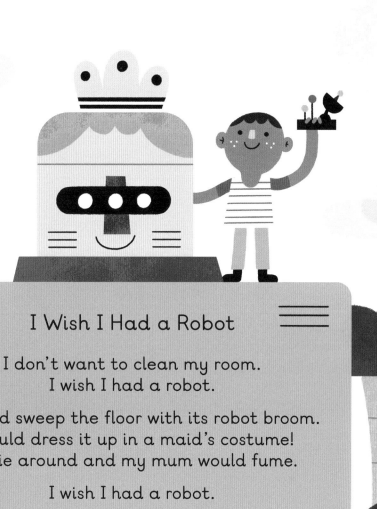

I Wish I Had a Robot

I don't want to clean my room.
I wish I had a robot.

It would sweep the floor with its robot broom.
I could dress it up in a maid's costume!
I'd lie around and my mum would fume.

I wish I had a robot.

What is a robot?

There are lots of things that people don't want to do. Luckily, there are robots that will do these jobs for us!

Four-legged robots can help soldiers carry equipment over rough ground.

A robot vacuum can clean the floor by itself!

Dull and difficult

Some chores are hard work, or just plain dull. But for a robot, there is no such thing as boring! They are strong and can do the same task over and over again.

6

Delicate

Some jobs, such as performing surgery, are important to get just right. A robot never gets tired or sloppy, and its work is accurate every time.

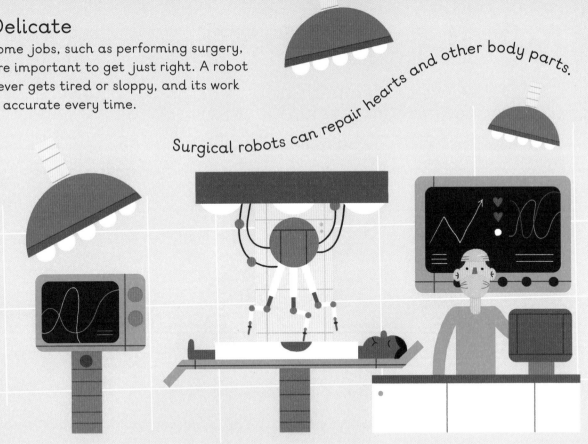

Surgical robots can repair hearts and other body parts.

Robots are often sent into dangerous situations.

Dangerous

People can't travel to Mars or go inside an active volcano. It's too dangerous. But a robot can! If a robot is destroyed, another one can be built.

Robots in history

For thousands of years, people all over the world have been attempting to create lifelike **machines** to serve us.

New York, USA

A robot called Elektro was shown at the 1939 World's Fair. It could walk and talk!

Illinois, USA

In 1900, the book *The Wonderful Wizard of Oz* featured the Tin Woodman, a mechanical man built to chop trees in the land of Oz.

Italy

In 1495, Leonardo da Vinci designed an amazing mechanical knight. It could sit up, wave its arms, and move its head.

What's in a name?

In the play *Rossum's Universal Robots*, first performed in 1921, Czech playwright Karel Capek introduced the term "robot" to describe a mechanical servant. *Robot* comes from the Czech word *robota*, which means "forced labour".

Greece
According to myth, the Greek god Hephaestus built a giant bronze robot to protect the island of Crete.

China
Legend says that King Mu was given a life-sized mechanical figure shaped like a human. It walked around and even sang!

India
In Indian legend, King Ajatashatru used mechanical men to guard holy items.

Egypt
In ancient Egypt, one palace was full of mechanical statues. Legend says they were so lifelike that people thought they had souls!

Middle East
In the land that is now Turkey, Ismail al-Jazari built mechanical musicians in the early 1200s. They were powered by water.

What makes a robot?

Robots are complicated! Here are some of the most common robot parts.

Robot tools

Each robot part has a different job. Tools called **sensors** help the robot make sense of the world around it. Movable parts like arms or wheels allow it to do its job. Inside is a **processor**. This mechanical "brain" takes in the instructions and then tells the robot's parts what to do.

tools for mapping its environment

GPS for pinpointing its location

a computer for planning and carrying out its **program**

cameras for seeing the world around it

arms for reaching

Robot parts

Believe it or not, a lot of the parts that make up a robot are things you can find right where you live.

Everyday objects

If you take a tour of your home, you'll see many items that can be used as robot parts. Here are some of the things you might find.

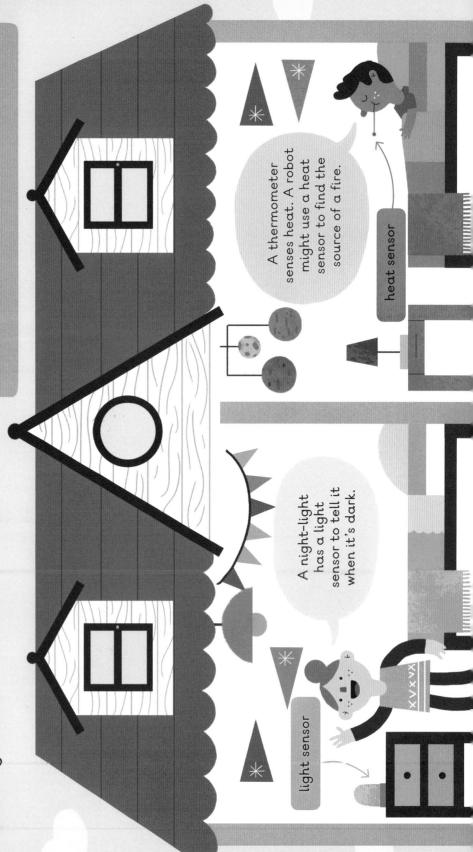

A thermometer senses heat. A robot might use a heat sensor to find the source of a fire.

heat sensor

A night-light has a light sensor to tell it when it's dark.

light sensor

tracks

A dial can control an oven – and a robot too!

Tracks like those on a toy tank would help a robot move across uneven ground.

dial

Bicycles have wheels and **gears**, just like some robots do!

gears

The motor in a vacuum cleaner could power a robot.

motor

Some of the parts you found might work as sensors. Others might be better for building a robot's body.

wheels

Building bodies

Robots can look very different. Each robot's body is designed for a particular task.

Mechanical arms

A robot assembling cars in a factory has a single task to perform, over and over. It doesn't need a human-like body, just an arm on a platform.

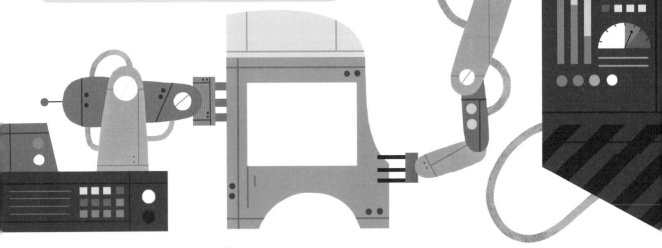

Tough tracks

Some robots are designed to travel over rubble or uneven ground. They might have treaded tracks like a tank.

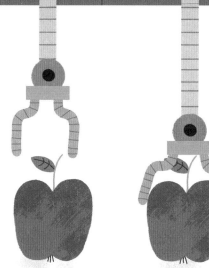

Gentle grippers

Robotic fingers for handling delicate fruit need to be soft, so they don't bruise the flesh. They can be made of soft plastics or even **gelatin** and water!

Micro-robots

Super-small robots can be swallowed like a pill. They go through the body to make repairs, take pictures or deliver medicine.

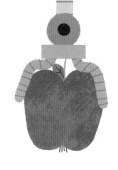

When a pill robot's job is done, it ends up in the toilet!

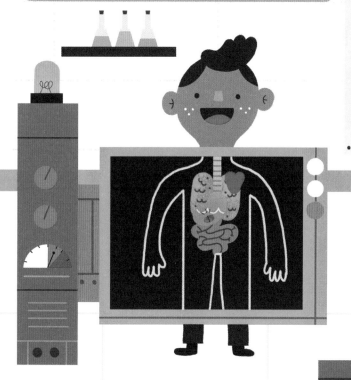

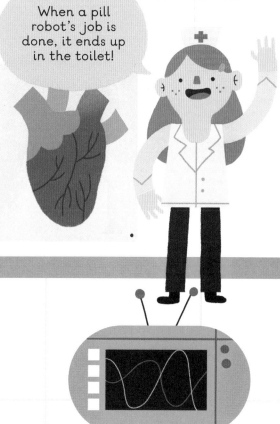

Bio-bots

Animals are amazing! Many robot designs are inspired by animals and what they can do.

A six-legged robot can easily move over uneven ground, just like an insect does.

Snakelike robots have bodies made of pieces connected by joints. They can slither through narrow passages.

Some robots are built like fish so they can swim through water.

With the right program, robots can act together, like a swarm of bees or a flock of birds.

Other robots are shaped like humans so they can move around our homes and our offices. Some can even climb stairs.

Robots built to look like people are called **androids**.

Make a robot costume

What do you think a robot looks like? Use everyday items to create a robot costume.

Tool kit

- cardboard box large enough to fit over your **torso**
- scissors
- plastic bottle caps
- coloured felt-tip pens
- foil
- non-toxic glue
- tape
- other odds and ends you could use for dials, knobs, and switches
- an adult to help

What to do

1 Assemble the cardboard box. Leave one end open. Set it on a table so that the open end is down.

2 Carefully cut off the flaps.

3 Ask an adult to cut a circular hole in the closed top of the box. Make sure it's big enough for your head to fit through comfortably.

4. Ask an adult to cut holes in the sides for your arms.

5. Try it on. Does it fit? Enlarge the holes until the box sits neatly on your shoulders and your arms can move freely.

6. Now it's time to use foil, felt-tip pens and more for decorating!

Use felt-tip pens to draw designs, or cover it with foil to look metallic.

Will your robot need lots of controls? Use bottle tops to create buttons and knobs.

Try this...
When creating your robot costume, remember that every robot is designed for a specific job. What will your robot's job be? As you add to your costume, try to think of an explanation for what each button, dial or switch is for.

Robotic hand

Have you ever wanted a robot hand? Build one out of household items, and then test its strength!

What to do

1 Take the wire hanger and bring the two sides together to form a shape like fingers of a hand.

Ask an adult if you need help bending the hanger.

Tool kit

- wire clothes hanger
- wooden dowel (at least 1 metre long)
- duct tape
- plastic pipe (approximately 2.5 cm diameter x 1 m long)
- rubber bands
- things to grab, such as a piece of paper, stuffed animal, drinks tin, book, tomato

2 Ask an adult to straighten out the hooked part of the hanger. That's the part that hangs over the rod in your wardobe.

3 Use duct tape to attach a wooden dowel to the straightened hook.

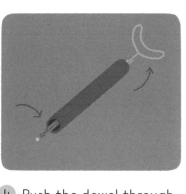

4 Push the dowel through the plastic pipe. The wire "fingers" should poke out of one end of the pipe and the dowel should poke out of the other.

5 Give your hand a gripping surface by wrapping rubber bands or duct tape around the end of each finger.

6 Pull on the dowel to make the fingers of the hand come together. Push on the dowel to release them.

What can your mechanical hand pick up around the house?

What happens?

Can you pick up a piece of paper? How about a book or a tomato? You'll find that your grabber works better for some items than for others. It is not as delicate and finely controlled as your fingers. Can you think of any ways to improve your grabber?

Sense, think, act

Robots follow a set of instructions called a program. But the most advanced robots can sense, think and act.

Think about it

Robots are more like you than you may realize. How do you know to carry an umbrella when it is raining? You see or hear the rain. You decide an umbrella will keep you dry. You grab an umbrella. Like you, a robot can sense, think and act. First it gathers **data**. Next, it makes a plan, and then acts on that plan.

Sense

First, the robot uses its sensors to gather information about its surroundings. Cameras, microphones and GPS are types of sensors. So are **radar** or **lidar**, which send out signals and wait for them to bounce back. Other sensors measure pressure and heat.

There's something in my way!

Think

Next, the robot's computer puts together all the data. It makes a picture of the world around it. Then it makes a plan. It figures out the best way to carry out its instructions.

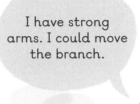

I have strong arms. I could move the branch.

Act

Finally, its body acts on its plan. It moves where it needs to go. It lifts what it needs to lift.

Imagine this!

A **rover** is exploring the surface of Mars. It is too far away to rely on human **commands**. Its program tells it to travel in a certain path, but there is a rock in the way. The robot uses its sensors to scan the area. Its computer uses that information to find a safe path. Then its body will travel on the new path.

Seeing and touching

A robot needs to know what its world looks like. Then it can move around safely.

Sensors

A robot's sensors act like its eyes and ears. Different sensors sense different things. They can sense objects, sounds, pressure or heat. Without sensors, a robot could not find a safe path.

Robot **vacuum cleaners** use sensors to find their way around your house. They move across the floor until they sense something in their way. Then they change direction. It's not very **efficient**, but sooner or later everything gets done.

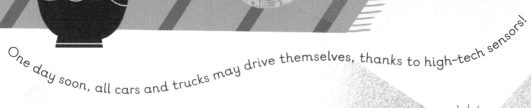

One day soon, all cars and trucks may drive themselves, thanks to high-tech sensors!

Sensors keep a **self-driving car** safe. Cameras scan the road to keep track of lane markings and other cars. They also read signs, so the car knows when to stop. GPS helps the car know where it is. It also helps plan the best way for getting where you want to go.

A **search-and-rescue** robot finds people trapped in collapsed buildings. Lidar lets it "see" in the dark. Heat sensors detect a victim's body heat, and microphones listen out for voices.

A robotic **planetary rover** might have cameras and GPS as well as lidar or radar. It may have a grasping hand that senses pressure. If a rock is in a robot's way, the robot will use its sensors to find a clear path around it.

Lidar uses **laser** beams to locate an object. Radar uses radio waves!

Act like a robot

Sensors are very important for robots. Find out how to get a robot to "think" and act.

Tool kit

- items to create an obstacle course, such as chairs, cushions or boxes
- a friend
- blindfold

What to do

1 First, set up an obstacle course in a safe place in your home or garden. Create simple, narrow paths with some twists and turns.

2 Ask a friend to act as a robot.

3 Blindfold your friend and set them at the entrance to the obstacle course.

Turn left.

4 Give step-by-step instructions for your friend to follow. Do it one move at a time, to avoid accidents.

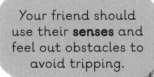

Your friend should use their **senses** and feel out obstacles to avoid tripping.

5 Once your friend finishes the course, talk about which instructions were helpful and which ones were not.

6 Switch roles. Let your friend create a new obstacle course. This time you follow their commands!

What happens?

Your friend is a remote-controlled robot and you are the controller. Your friend's senses take the place of a real robot's mechanical sensors. The sense of hearing lets your friend listen to your instructions. The sense of touch alerts them to any items that may be blocking their path.

Try this...

Why not create a storyline for your obstacle course? For example, your friend could pretend to be a search-and-rescue robot finding its way through a collapsed building.

Sound clues

You have sound sensors, just like a robot! Try using your ears to figure out the location and distance of the sounds around you.

Tool kit

- a friend
- chair (optional)
- blindfold
- pencil
- sound clues record sheet

What to do

1. Have a friend sit in a chair or on the floor. Put a blindfold on them.

2. Stand either behind, beside or in front of your friend. You should be either one or three steps away. Now make a noise, such as clapping your hands.

3. Ask your friend to guess the direction of the sound and whether it came from near or far. Try a variety of locations, distances and sounds. Each time, make a note of where you were and what you did, as well as their guesses.

4 Switch places with your friend and repeat the procedure.

How well did your sound sensors work?

What happens?

Look at your record sheet. Do you see any patterns? Were some noises easier to locate than others? Were some locations easier to identify?

Sound clues record sheet

Location	Noise	Distance	Location correct?	Distance correct?
front	moo	one step	no	yes
back	snap	three steps	yes	yes

Did you know?

A robot can use sound to map its surroundings. It sends out sound waves, which bounce back when they hit an object. The robot's sensors pick up the sound waves when they return. The robot's computer measures how long it took for the waves to get there. This tells it how far away the object is. The robot uses this information to create a clear picture of its environment.

When robots use sound waves to gather information, it is called **sonar**.

Robot antennae

Many robots have **antennae**. Make your own pair of robot antennae and find out what these slim rods are for.

Tool kit

- metallic pipe cleaners
- child-sized plastic headband
- cool-melt glue gun
- an adult to help

What to do

Glue can be messy! Use some old newspapers to protect your table.

1. Take a metallic pipe cleaner and centre it over the middle of the headband. Then glue it in place. (An adult should be in charge of using the glue gun.)

2. Take two more pipe cleaners and put a bend in them about a third of the way down. Take the shorter end and glue it to the side of the headband, right where the first pipe cleaner ends.

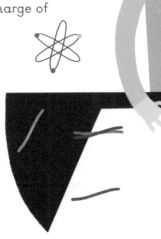

3 When the glue has cooled, bend the free ends of the pipe cleaners away from the headband. Then bend the ends into whatever shape you like.

Sensing tools

Antennae are great for sensing, but these slim rods are not the only sensing tool that robot designers use. Robots can have cameras, lasers, GPS and sonar. They can also have sensors that detect things such as pressure and temperature.

Touch clues

Try sensing like a robot to identify the secret object hidden inside a bag.

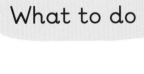
What to do

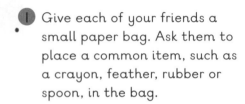

Tool kit

- several friends
- small paper bags
- pencils
- small items to place in the bags
- touch clues record sheets

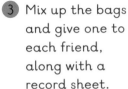

1 Give each of your friends a small paper bag. Ask them to place a common item, such as a crayon, feather, rubber or spoon, in the bag.

2 Have each friend write their name on the bag. Then fold the top of the bag shut.

Make sure you don't give someone their own bag!

3 Mix up the bags and give one to each friend, along with a record sheet.

Alex

Jamal

Flynn

No peeking allowed!

4 Investigate the bag. You can do this by lifting the bag, shaking it gently, feeling it on the outside or smelling it. You can even use a pencil to touch the item inside, as long as you don't look in the bag.

5 Write down each observation on your record sheet. Try to guess what is in the bag and write down your idea.

6 Once you've finished your investigation, open the bag to see what is inside.

Property to explore	Method of sensing	Discovery	Guess
shape	touched bag	long and thin	string
weight	lifted bag	heavier than a rope	pencil
size			
texture			
odour			
sound			

What happens?

Robots use their sensors to gather information on an unknown object's features. Then they compare it to facts about objects they have been programmed to recognize. Each matched fact is a clue the robot can use to identify the object.

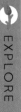

Computers and programs

At the heart of every robot is a computer. This computer is the thinking part of the machine.

Programs

The computer in a robot runs a program. A program is the set of instructions that a robot must follow to do its job. These instructions are very detailed, so there is no room for error. A robot's program can be changed or replaced by another program.

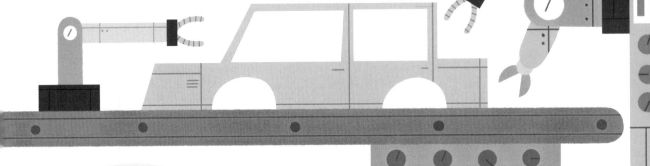

A robot in a car factory might be programmed to screw pieces of metal together.

Robot code

The instructions that make up a program are called **code**. Code is made by taking simple commands, like "start", and stringing them together. Something like "if the gas tank is full, then start" is a line of code. A program that adds two numbers together is simple, so it would only need a few lines of code. But a program that lets a robot recognize a face is much longer and more complicated.

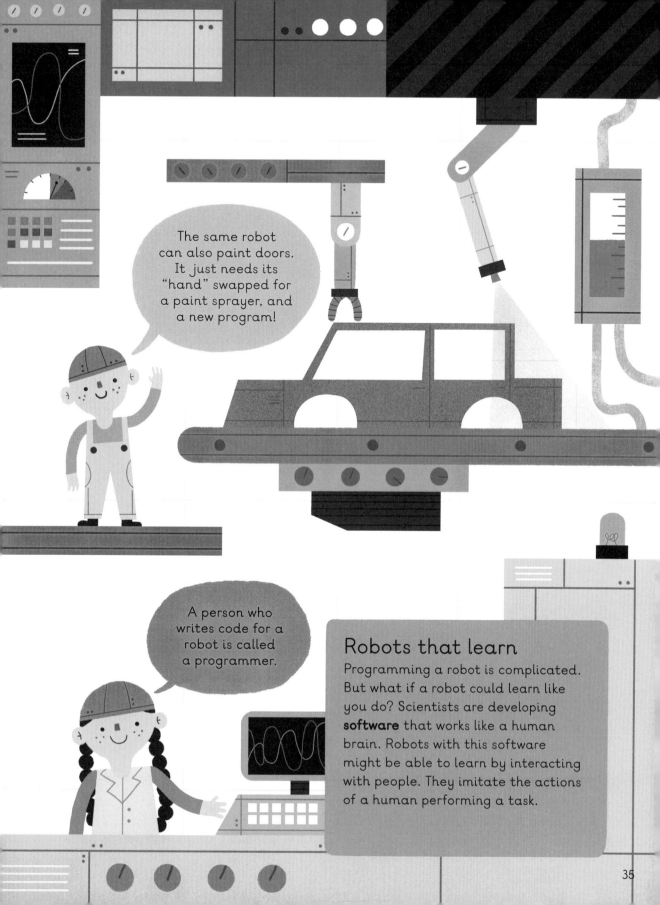

The same robot can also paint doors. It just needs its "hand" swapped for a paint sprayer, and a new program!

A person who writes code for a robot is called a programmer.

Robots that learn

Programming a robot is complicated. But what if a robot could learn like you do? Scientists are developing **software** that works like a human brain. Robots with this software might be able to learn by interacting with people. They imitate the actions of a human performing a task.

Run a simple program

You can run a program just like a robot would. All you need is a group of friends.

Tool kit

- three or more people
- record sheet
- pencil

What to do

1. You're going to sort your friends by height. Ask them to line up in a random order. Record the number of people on your record sheet.

2. Start by comparing the pair of people on the left. Is the person on the left taller than the one on the right? If so, then swap their positions.

Number of people	|||
Number of comparisons	
Number of swaps	
Number of times you go through the line	

3. Keep track of how many comparisons and swaps you make by putting a tally on the record sheet each time.

4. Now compare the pair immediately to the right and repeat the process. Keep going until you reach the end of the line.

5. Go back to the pair on the left and repeat these steps until no one needs to swap positions. Each time you start over at the beginning of the line, mark it on your record sheet.

What happens?

You have just run a sorting program! A computer would follow the same process if it were sorting numbers into order. There are many ways to sort. This one is called "bubble sort". Why? Because the largest, or tallest, item "bubbles" to the top.

You could use this "bubble" method to sort your friends by age instead of height. You could also sort objects by size or colour.

37

Robot sandwich

It's time to turn your friend into a robot. If you do a good job, you may end up with a tasty snack!

Tool kit

- record sheet
- a friend to help
- sliced cheese
- two slices of bread

What to do

1   On the record sheet, write down the steps needed to make a simple cheese sandwich. Add as many lines as you need.

STEP	RESULT	ADJUSTMENT
1. extend right arm forward		
2. grasp bread		

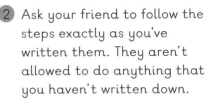

2   Ask your friend to follow the steps exactly as you've written them. They aren't allowed to do anything that you haven't written down.

3 How far did your friend get before there was a problem? Record the error and make a new plan. Then rewrite the instructions, and try again.

STEP	RESULT	ADJUSTMENT
1. extend right arm forward	arm extended past food	add additional step: lower arm until it touches bread
2. grasp bread	since arm was extended past food in step 1, the bread is now too far below arm	

Yum!

What happens?

You will soon realize that it is not enough to ask your friend to reach for the cheese. You must be very specific. How far should they extend their arm? Should they angle it up or down? How much? When should they use their fingers to grab? When should they let go?

Creating programs

Many programs are created by writing a set of detailed instructions. But they can also be created by simply guiding a robot through a task. The robot "remembers" the motion and then recreates it later.

What other tasks could you program your friend to do?

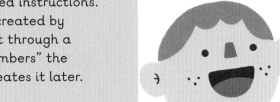

Escape the maze!

Help! Can you unscramble the code to help the lost robot escape the maze?

What to do

1. Use the commands listed in the "Commands" box to move the robot from the centre of the maze to the exit marked "A". You must follow the rules in the "Rules" box below.

2. Use the same commands to get the robot out through exits B, C and D. You'll need to order them differently!

Rules

1. You can use each command as many times as needed.

2. You can arrange the commands in any order.

3. The robot can only move in the direction it is facing.

4. To exit, the robot needs to be standing on the door block and facing in the direction of the arrow.

EXIT C

EXIT B

EXIT A

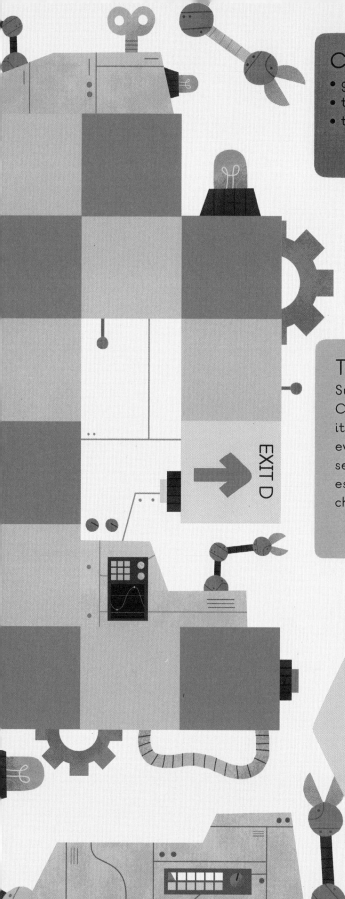

Commands
- go forwards one square
- turn left
- turn right

Wow! I just wrote a program!

Try this...
Suppose the robot carried a paintbrush. Can you write a program that will make it draw a T? How about an L? You could even try making your own maze, then see if a friend can write commands to escape it. Try adding different challenges and different commands.

EXIT D

How did you do?
Here is the fastest sequence of steps to get out through exit A.

- Go forwards one square
- Go forwards one square
- Turn right
- Go forwards one square
- Turn left
- Go forwards one square

Artificial intelligence

Robots that do jobs are useful. But can we design robots that are actually intelligent?

What is intelligence?

Intelligence is the ability to learn knowledge and skills and then apply them. You are intelligent. Your pets are intelligent, too. But what does it mean for a machine to be intelligent? And how can we tell if it is?

Natural or artificial?

You and other animals are "naturally intelligent". When a computer or robot mimics human-like intelligence, we call that **artificial intelligence**, or AI for short.

The Turing test

A scientist named Alan Turing came up with a test to tell if a machine is artificially intelligent. In the Turing Test, a tester sits at a keyboard and starts two chat sessions. One session is with an AI, and the other is with a real person. The tester cannot see the person or AI they are chatting with.

Asking questions

The tester asks and answers questions with the person and the AI. They discuss a variety of topics. The tester does not know which is the computer or which is the human.

WHAT IS YOUR FAVORITE COLOUR?

I LIKE GREEN BEST.

Decision time!

At the end of the test, the tester guesses which chat session was with the human. If the tester can't tell the difference and picks the AI, then the AI has successfully mimicked human intelligence.

If you were the tester, what questions would you ask?

Did you know?

In 2014, an AI first passed the Turing Test. It was a piece of software that pretends to be a 13-year-old boy!

Dealing with robots

Even if a robot can think like a person, it might still seem scary. How would you make a robot seem more friendly?

I'd give it a face!

Maybe it could look like me!

How about a mouth that can smile?

Robot faces

Robot designers are working to make robots that look like people. They put a **silicone** skin over the metal parts. They sculpt and paint the material to look like a person's face. Then they program the robot with different expressions.

This robot has a program that allows it to recognize faces. When it sees a human face...

its eyes crinkle...

its lips smile...

Scientists have proved that many people prefer robots with female voices.

and it says hello...

Hello, Robot!

Hello, Clare!

Think about it

Some people feel uncomfortable around robots that look too much like a real person. Would you rather talk to a robot that looks like a machine or one that looks like a person?

Feelings bot

Robots don't have real emotions. But you can make a feelings bot that looks like it does!

Tool kit

- copy of feelings bot face (see template on pages 60–61)
- scissors
- copy of eye, eyebrow and mouth strips (see template on pages 60–61)

What to do

1 Trace or photocopy the feelings bot face template.

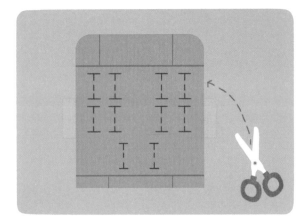

2 Carefully cut along the dotted lines to give the face a series of slits.

3 Cut out the strips for eyes, eyebrows and mouth. (The different features on these strips will let you give your robot facial expressions.)

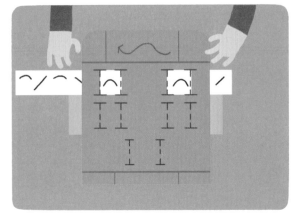

4 Weave the eyebrow strip through the top row of slots in the face. Go up through one slit and back down through the next. When you're finished, you should see two eyebrows on the face.

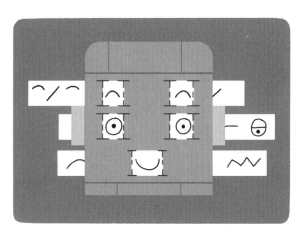

5 Weave the eye strip through the middle row in the same way. Then weave the mouth strip through the bottom row.

6 Start programming the robot by sliding the strips backward and forward. **Experiment** with changing its expression to show different emotions.

What happens?

Each set of eyebrows, eyes and mouth is different. When they are combined, they make a unique expression. What combination of features makes the feelings bot look happy? Can you change one or more of the features to make it look angry or sad?

Try this...

What other emotions could your feelings bot show? You may want to draw new strips with different eyes, eyebrows and mouth. Gather some friends to look at the different combinations. How well they can guess its emotions?

Jobs for robots

Whether you realize it or not, robots are doing jobs around us every day.

Robots can clean windows, and even provide security at shopping malls!

Who needs real pets? A robotic toy dog is great for playing fetch.

Cars are built by factory robots. Self-driving cars are robots themselves!

Drones can be used to deliver objects. One day soon, a fleet of drones may bring packages to our homes.

Many people have had an operation performed by a surgical robot!

To keep their lawn looking neat and tidy, many people use a robotic lawnmower to cut the grass.

Some of the items in a pack lunch may have been packed by a robot.

Tricky work

Robots do jobs that are too dull, dirty, delicate or dangerous for people. Can you match each robot with its workplace?

Tough search and rescue robots can move easily over rubble or work in tight spaces. These robots are usually remote controlled. Cameras and microphones send video and audio back to its operators.

Rovers gather information and do experiments on the Moon and on other planets. Was there ever life on Mars? Could we live on the Moon? Robots will help us find out.

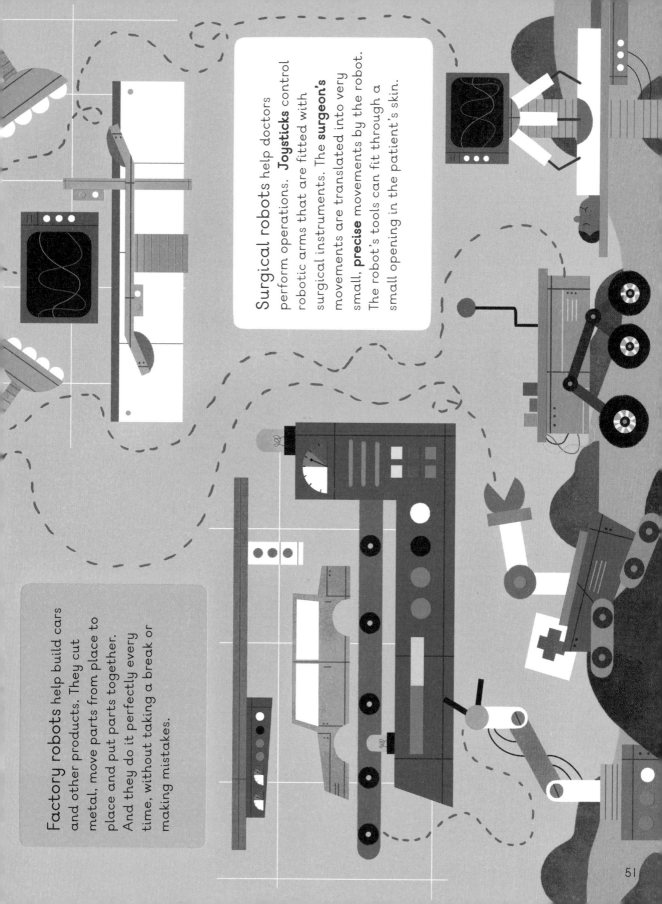

Surgical robots help doctors perform operations. **Joysticks** control robotic arms that are fitted with surgical instruments. The **surgeon's** movements are translated into very small, **precise** movements by the robot. The robot's tools can fit through a small opening in the patient's skin.

Factory robots help build cars and other products. They cut metal, move parts from place to place and put parts together. And they do it perfectly every time, without taking a break or making mistakes.

Space explorers

Lots of robots work in space. Here are just a few of them.

Why send robots?

Space is not an easy place for humans to survive. Astronauts need a **pressurized** suit to protect their bodies. They need air, water and food. But travelling in space is much easier for a robot. As long as it has power and a program, it's good to go.

Voyager

Voyager 1 is a robotic spacecraft. It is the farthest man-made object from Earth, but it still receives and uses new programs. It has sent back pictures of Jupiter and Saturn and gathered information about their moons, their weather and their rings. It has been in space for more than 40 years!

Can you think of any places on Earth where it might be safer to send robots to explore, instead of people?

What other dangerous jobs do you think robots could be used for?

Space station

The International Space Station (ISS) has a robotic arm called Canadarm2. This arm helped build the ISS by adding new parts. Now it is used to grab or release **satellites**. It can even help move astronauts when they do spacewalks!

Robonaut

Robonaut also works on the ISS. This robot looks like a human torso. It has hands and arms, and it uses the same tools as people use. It helps astronauts keep the space station in working order.

Mars Rover

Curiosity is a planetary rover. It is studying the rocks and climate on Mars. It can take samples of the Martian soil and do experiments. The data it gathers helps scientists learn more about Mars. Curiosity may even find signs of past life on Mars!

Pasta rover

Make your own planetary rover out of pasta. Then send it on a mission into space – or maybe just your living room!

Tool kit

- paper and pencil
- different pasta shapes, including rotelle (wheel-shaped), spaghetti, penne, bow ties and lasagna
- cold-melt glue gun
- paint, glitter and other things for decorating
- flat piece of metal, wood or heavy plastic, to make a ramp
- books to raise the ramp up at one end

What to do

1 Lay out your pasta and make a plan. How could you use the different shapes to build a rover? Sketch your ideas on a piece of paper.

2 Start with a flat sheet of lasagna and then add other types of pasta to build the rover's body. Use the glue gun to connect the pieces of pasta to each other.

3 Add special features, such as a bow tie to represent a camera, or a robotic arm made of spaghetti.

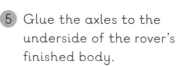

4 Thread spaghetti through the holes in your rotelle "wheels". Make sure the wheels spin freely on their spaghetti axles.

5 Glue the axles to the underside of the rover's finished body.

6 Use paint, markers, and glitter to decorate your pasta rover.

Try this...

Place one end of a flat piece of wood (or plastic or metal) on the floor. Place the other end on a tower of books to make a ramp. Make sure there's space at the bottom of your ramp so your rover can keep on rolling. Place your pasta rover at the top of the ramp and let it go!

Invite a friend to make a rover, then have a race. Which rover rolls the fastest?

Be a robot designer

Robots are made to do jobs that humans don't want to do. What job would you design a robot for?

Tool kit

- paper
- pencil
- crayons or coloured pencils

A robot would make life much easier!

What to do

1 Think of a job that you do often but don't like very much. It might be making your bed, laying the table or folding washing.

2 Think about how you could design a robot to do the job for you. What would it need? Cameras to see? Would it move on wheels, treads, feet or something else? Would it have an arm? One or two?

3 Draw a picture of your robot. Make sure to include its name and what materials it is made of. Don't forget to label the sensors it uses and make a note of how it moves.

Build a robot

Make a fun toy that looks like a robot and moves on its own, too!

Tool kit

- sheet of **foamcore**
- scissors
- cool-melt glue gun
- 3v motor
- AA battery
- paperclips or toothbrush heads
- electrical tape
- two pieces of rubber-coated electrical wire, each 7 to 13 cm long
- beads, googly eyes or other trimmings
- an adult to help

What to do

1 Cut a piece of foamcore that just fits the size of the motor.

2 Use glue to attach it to the motor, so that the metal contacts are on top.

3 Glue the battery to the motor.

4 Glue a bead or a small piece of foamcore onto one end of the motor.

5 Fold paperclips to make the legs. Glue them to the piece of foamcore.

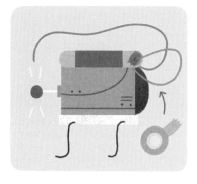

6 Ask an adult to help you to twist the wires onto the metal **contacts** on the motor.

7 Attach the end of one of the wires to one end of your battery with electrical tape.

8 Give your robot some personality. Use hot glue to attach eyes, nose, antennae, and any other trimmings.

9 Take your second wire and tape it to the non-wired end of the battery. Set your robot toy on a flat surface and watch it move!

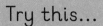

Try this...

If you want your robot to have a lot of legs, try a toothbrush head! Ask an adult to cut the head off a toothbrush and use hot glue to attach it to the foamcore.

Templates

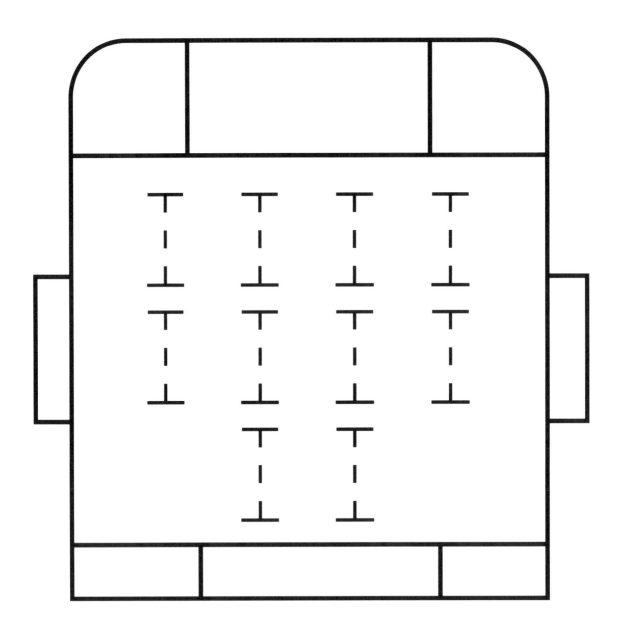

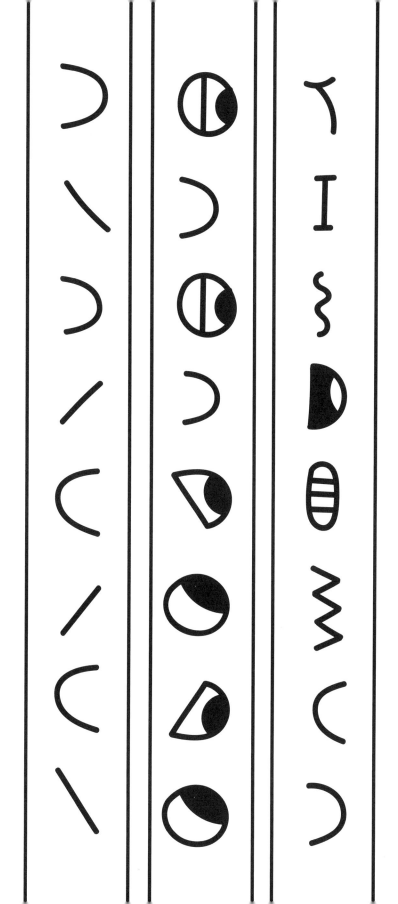

Glossary

Android A robot built to resemble a human being

Antennae A device used for sensing or for sending or receiving radio signals

Artificial intelligence The ability of a machine to imitate intelligent human behaviour

Code A set of instructions for a computer

Command An order

Contacts Places where surfaces touch, allowing an electrical current to pass through

Data Facts that can be used in calculating, reasoning or planning

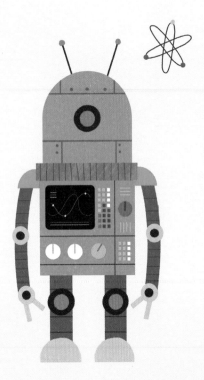

Drone An aircraft or ship without a pilot that is controlled by radio signals

Efficient Capable of producing the desired results with a minimum of wasted energy or material

Experiment A procedure carried out to discover something or test an idea

Foamcore A stiff but lightweight board made of foam and covered on both sides with paper

Gears Toothed wheels that control a vehicle's speed and direction of travel

Gelatin A soft, gummy protein that is obtained by boiling animal tissues

GPS (short for Global Positioning System) A system that uses satellite signals to find the location of a radio receiver on or above Earth's surface

Joystick A handheld device used to control movement in a computer game or aircraft

Laser A device that makes a very narrow, powerful beam of light

Lidar A device that uses laser beams to detect and locate objects

Machine A device made up of moving parts that use forces, motion and energy to do a desired task

Precise Accurate and exact

Pressure The application of force to something by something else in direct contact with it

Pressurized Adapted to maintain air pressure at a level similar to that on Earth

Processor The part of a computer that processes data

Program A set of step-by-step instructions that tell a computer to do something with data

Radar A device that uses radio waves to detect and locate objects

Rover A mobile exploration robot designed to move over rough ground

Satellite A man-made object or vehicle intended to orbit Earth, the Moon or another heavenly body

Senses Abilities that allow a person to be aware of their surroundings

Sensor An instrument that can detect a change in something like heat, sound or pressure

Silicone A soft, man-made material used to simulate human skin

Software The programs and related information used by a computer

Sonar A device that uses sound waves to detect and locate things underwater

Surgeon A doctor who is trained to perform operations

Torso The human body except for the head, arms and legs

Tracks The metal belts on which a vehicle, such as a bulldozer, travels

Treaded Having a textured part on a wheel, tyre, or track that makes contact with a road, or other surface

Index

Now that you are a robot expert, see how many robots you can spot in the world around you!

Quarto is the authority on a wide range of topics.

Quarto educates, entertains and enriches the lives of our readers—enthusiasts and lovers of hands-on living.

www.quartoknows.com

Author: Jenny Fretland VanVoorst
Illustrator: Pau Morgan
Consultant: Dave Hawksett
Editors: Nancy Dickmann, Ellie Brough
Designer: Clare Barber

© 2018 Quarto Publishing plc

First published in 2018 by QED Publishing, an imprint of The Quarto Group.
The Old Brewery, 6 Blundell Street,
London, N7 9BH, United Kingdom.
T (0)20 7700 6700 F (0)20 7700 8066
www.QuartoKnows.com

ISBN 978 1 78493 560 3

9 8 7 6 5 4 3 2 1

Manufactured in Dongguan, China
TL032018

MIX
Paper from responsible sources
FSC® C104723
www.fsc.org